Rude Little Reggie WANTS A PET

Michael Wagner

Illustrated by Pablo Márquez

Rude Little Reggie is rude to everyone and everything. And he never learns his lesson.

Once, he even said to his mum, "I want a pet! Get me one now!"

Reggie's mum was shocked, but she was also very clever. So she replied, "You can have a pet if you promise to mow the lawn."

"I'll never do chores!" declared Reggie.

"Then, no pets for you," said his mum.

Reggie was also clever, so he thought of a plan to get a pet without having to mow the lawn.

"If you give me the pet I want, the lawn will always be mowed," he said to his mum. "I promise."

The next day, Reggie's mother bought him the pet he wanted . . . a sheep.

Shirley the sheep chewed the lawn and kept the grass nice and short.

"Now I have a pet and I will never have to mow the lawn," said Reggie. "Perfect!"

And it was perfect, until…

“I’m bored with Shirley the sheep,” Reggie told his mum. “I need another pet!”

His mum thought for a moment, then replied, “Okay, but only if you promise to do the dishes.”

"Okay," agreed Reggie. "I promise."

The next day, Reggie's mum bought him a pet octopus.

“Now I have a new pet and I will never have to do the dishes,” said Reggie. “Perfect!”

And it was perfect, until …

“I’m bored with Olive the octopus,” Reggie told his mum. “I need a new pet! And make it a good one this time!”

His mum thought for a moment, then replied, "Okay, but only if you promise to wash the car."

The next day, Reggie's mum bought him a pet elephant.

"Now I have a new pet and I will never have to wash the car," said Reggie. "Perfect!"

And it was perfect, until …

"I'm bored with Ernie the elephant," Reggie announced to his mum. "In fact, I'm bored with all of my pets!"

"How rude!" said Shirley the sheep.

"After all we've done for you!" cried Olive the octopus.

"We're leaving!" declared Ernie the elephant.

Later that day, the pet shop van arrived at Reggie's house. The pets climbed into the back as quickly as they could.

“Good!” said Reggie. “I don’t need boring pets anyway!”

"Reggie!" called his mum.
"The lawn needs mowing and the dishes are dirty! The car could use a wash, too! Don't forget, you promised!"

"Come back, pets!" cried Reggie. "I'm sor … I'm sorr …"

"I'm SORRY!" cried Reggie. "I won't be rude any more!"

But it was too late. His pets had gone.

Reggie had finally learnt his lesson …

or had he?

“Boring lawn!”
“Boring dishes!”
“Boring car!”